Creative Machines

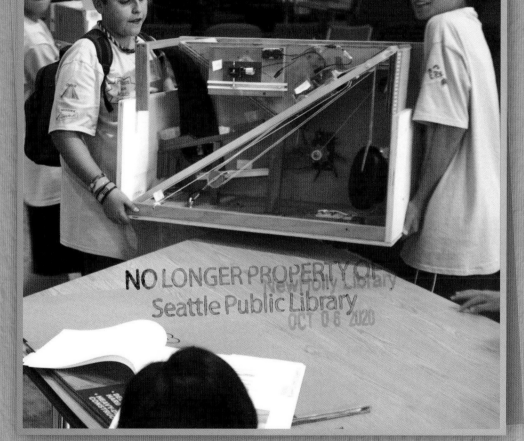

Dona Herweck Rice

✳ Smithsonian

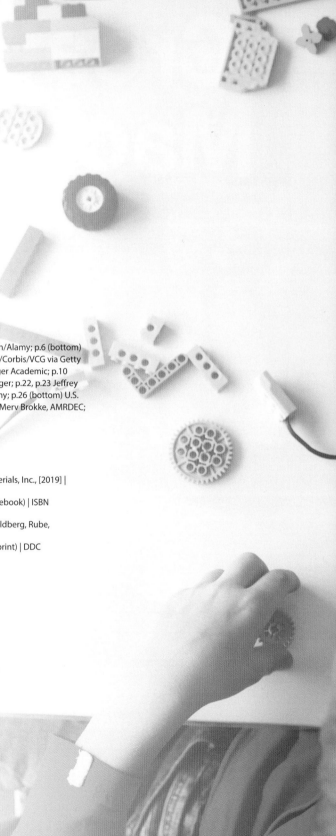

Contributing Author

Jennifer Lawson

Consultants

Tim Pula
Interpretive Exhibit Coordinator
Spark!Lab, Lemelson Center
National Museum of American History

Sharon Banks
3rd Grade Teacher
Duncan Public Schools

Publishing Credits

Rachelle Cracchiolo, M.S.Ed., *Publisher*
Conni Medina, M.A.Ed., *Managing Editor*
Diana Kenney, M.A.Ed., NBCT, *Content Director*
Véronique Bos, *Creative Director*
Robin Erickson, *Art Director*
Michelle Jovin, M.A., *Associate Editor*
Mindy Duits, *Senior Graphic Designer*
Smithsonian Science Education Center

Image Credits: front cover, p.1 David L. Moore - Education/Alamy; p.6 (bottom) Library of Congress [LC-DIG-npcc-17319]; p.7 Oscar White/Corbis/VCG via Getty Images; p.8 Stamp Collection/Alamy; p.9 (top), p.11 Granger Academic; p.10 AP Photo/John Lindsay; p.18 (top) AP Photo/Dave Umberger; p.22, p.23 Jeffrey Coolidge/Getty Images; p.25 (top) Everett Collection/Alamy; p.26 (bottom) U.S. Air Force photo by Alex R. Lloyd; p.27 U.S. Army photo by Merv Brokke, AMRDEC; all other images from iStock and/or Shutterstock.

Library of Congress Cataloging-in-Publication Data

Names: Rice, Dona, author.
Title: Creative machines / Dona Herweck Rice.
Description: Huntington Beach, CA : Teacher Created Materials, Inc., [2019] | Audience: K to grade 3. | Includes index. |
Identifiers: LCCN 2018031132 (print) | LCCN 2018031926 (ebook) | ISBN 9781493869084 (E-book) | ISBN 9781493866687 (pbk.)
Subjects: LCSH: Machine desingn--Juvenile literature. | Goldberg, Rube, 1883-1970--Juvenile literature.
Classification: LCC TJ230 (ebook) | LCC TJ230 .R508 2020 (print) | DDC 621.8/15--dc23
LC record available at https://lccn.loc.gov/2018031132

Teacher Created Materials

5301 Oceanus Drive
Huntington Beach, CA 92649-1030
www.tcmpub.com
ISBN 978-1-4938-6668-7
© 2019 Teacher Created Materials, Inc.

Table of Contents

Build a Better Mousetrap

If you want to butter bread, you spread it with a knife. If you want to open a door, you turn the knob and push. If you want to catch a mouse, you set a trap and wait for it to spring. But is there a better way?

A famous phrase is: "Build a better mousetrap, and the world will beat a path to your door." It means that everyone will want what you made. But if a simple thing works well, is there always a better way?

This mousetrap can hurt a mouse.

This mousetrap does not hurt a mouse.

Hello, Rube!

On the Fourth of July in 1883, a baby boy was born. His name was Reuben Goldberg. People called him Rube (ROOB).

As a boy, Goldberg loved to draw. His father did not think drawing would get him far in life. He wanted Goldberg to become an **engineer**. So, that is what he studied in college. But his love of drawing did not go away.

Later, Goldberg left his high-paying job as an engineer. He became a **cartoonist**! He did not make much money, but it was work he wanted to do.

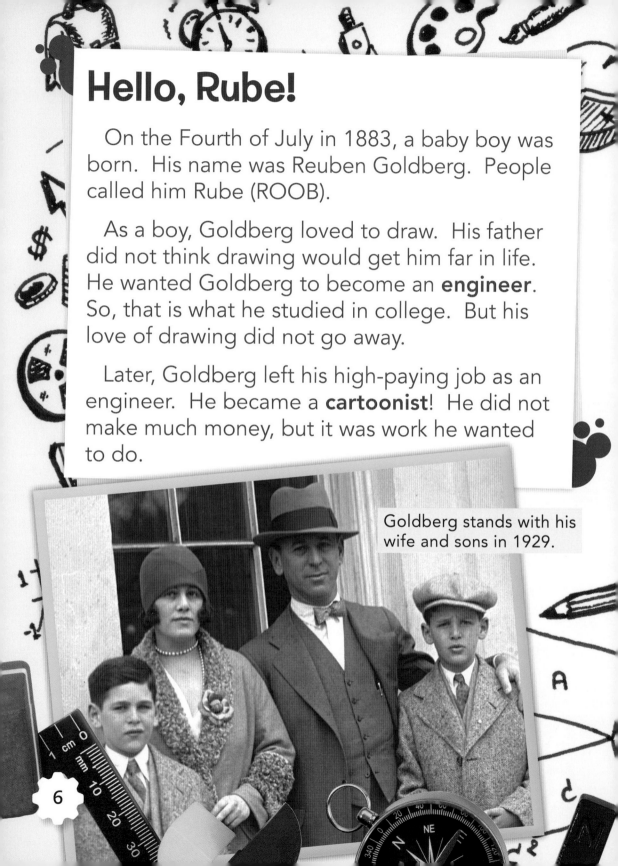

Goldberg stands with his wife and sons in 1929.

Goldberg in the 1940s

Goldberg drew a lot of comics. Some of them were about serious topics. They made people think. Other comics made people laugh. One of them even won a **Pulitzer Prize**!

Goldberg was also famous for his drawings of machines. The machines used tools to do simple tasks in **complex** ways. They made people laugh.

One of his most famous drawings was his napkin machine. Goldberg drew a complex way to use a napkin. It shows a series of causes and effects. The man uses the napkin but never has to pick it up.

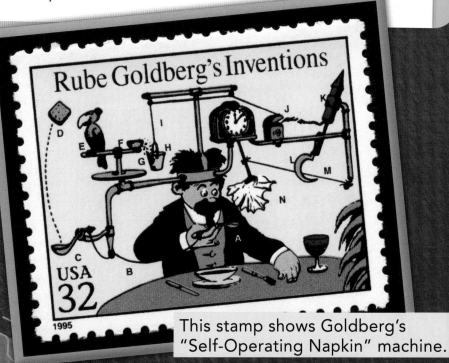

This stamp shows Goldberg's "Self-Operating Napkin" machine.

Technology & Engineering

Cause and Effect

Engineers think about cause and effect. They know moving water will turn a waterwheel. They know wind will turn a windmill. They must know each action has a reaction. That helps them know what to expect.

Goldberg draws his last cartoon in 1964.

Goldberg spent over 30 hours drawing each machine!

Goldberg's machines were famous. He drew each one with a character he named Professor Butts. Butts did easy things in hard ways. People could not wait to see what he would draw next.

People called his inventions Rube Goldberg Machines. The simpler the task, the more likely it would become one of his machines. Does someone need to scratch a bug bite? Butts can help. Does someone need to open a window? Butts can help with that too. There is even one to wash someone's back in a bathtub!

INVENTIONS OF PROFESSOR LUCIFER BUTTS

Professor Butts steps into an open elevator shaft and when he lands at the bottom he finds a simple orange squeezing machine. Milk man takes empty milk bottle (A) pulling string (B) which causes sword (C) to sever cord (D) and allow guillotine blade (E) to drop and cut rope (F) which releases battering ram (G). Ram bumps against open door (H) causing it to close. Grass sickle (I) cuts a slice off end of orange (J) at the same time spike (K) stabs "prune hawk" (L) he opens his mouth to yell in agony, thereby releasing prune and allowing diver's boot (M) to drop and step on sleeping octopus (N). Octopus awakens in a rage and seeing diver's face which is painted on orange, attacks it and crushes it with tentacles, thereby causing all the juice in the orange to run into glass (O).
Later on you can use the log to build a log cabin where you can raise your son to be president like Abraham Lincoln.

This Goldberg cartoon shows how to squeeze an orange.

Simple Machines

Goldberg's drawings are made of simple machines. Each action sets off the next. Once they are joined, they make one **compound** machine.

A simple machine makes work easier to do. It may change the power of a force. It may change its direction. It helps people do work with less effort. Heavy things can seem light. Simple machines make all these things possible.

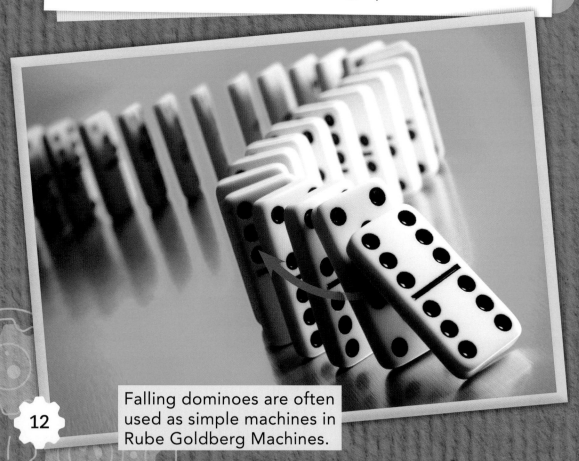

Falling dominoes are often used as simple machines in Rube Goldberg Machines.

The force of flowing water turns this waterwheel.

Feel the Force

Force is a push or pull on an object that comes from its interaction with another object. A person or a machine can apply a force. Things like wind and water can too. Rube Goldberg Machines work because forces are at work.

Pushes and Pulls

There are six types of simple machines. Each one uses pushes and/or pulls to do a task. All six can be sorted into one of two groups—levers or inclined planes. The lever group includes levers, wheels and axles, and pulleys.

A lever has a point of **balance**. A push or pull on one end can move a thing on the other end.

A wheel and axle is a type of lever. An object moves as the wheel is pushed, pulled, or turned.

A pulley is another type of lever. A rope or other object is pulled around the pulley to move something.

A seesaw is a type of lever.

point of balance

14

A point of balance is inside this metal pulley.

point of balance

point of balance

This wheel and axle has a point of balance.

15

A wedge uses two inclined planes to help break apart this wood.

A skater goes down an inclined plane.

The inclined plane group includes inclined planes, wedges, and screws. An inclined plane has a **sloping** surface. Something can be pushed or pulled along the plane.

A wedge is a type of inclined plane. Wedges can break things apart. They can also hold objects in place. They can even raise objects.

A screw is also a type of inclined plane. The inclined plane curls around a **shaft**. The inclined plane lifts or lowers objects when the screw turns. It also uses its inclined plane to hold objects together.

This screw has an inclined plane curled around it.

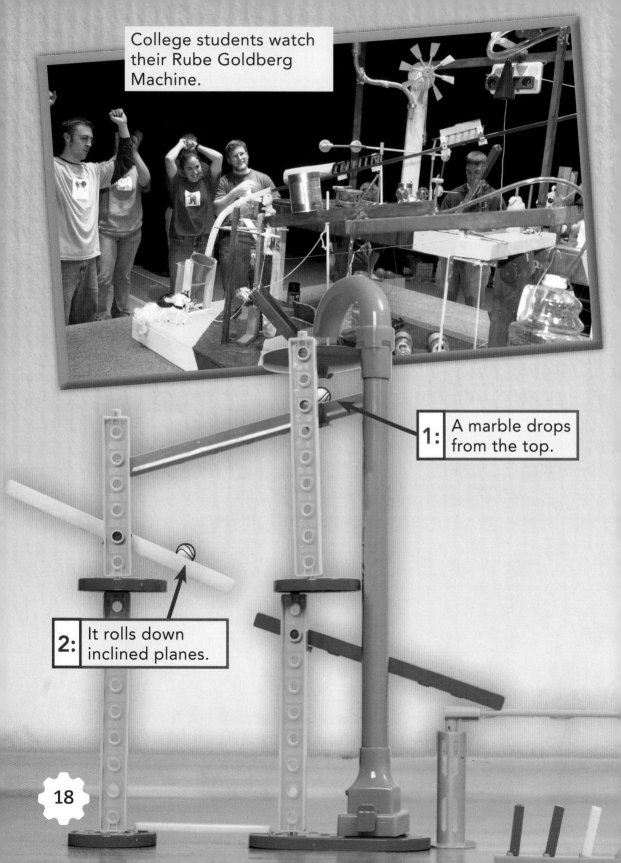

College students watch their Rube Goldberg Machine.

1: A marble drops from the top.

2: It rolls down inclined planes.

18

Yearly Contests

Rube Goldberg Machines are compound machines. People love to make them. In fact, there are Rube Goldberg Machine Contests every year. All **entrants** must be students. Each year, there is a new task to be done. One year, the machine had to hammer a nail. Another year, it had to zip a zipper. Another year, it had to build a burger!

There are rules for all entrants. The rules explain how many steps the machines should take. They also explain whether people can be part of the machines. Winners keep the spirit of Goldberg alive.

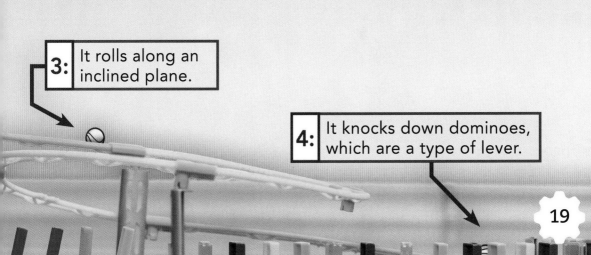

3: It rolls along an inclined plane.

4: It knocks down dominoes, which are a type of lever.

The first Rube Goldberg Machine Contest took place at a college. That was in 1949. Now, contests take place all over. First, teams compete in local contests. The winners of those contests can go to a **national** contest.

To win, a machine must work perfectly two out of three times. It must take a certain number of steps. Teamwork is also part of the score. If a machine gets stuck, a person can help. But the team will lose points. The machine should do the work on its own.

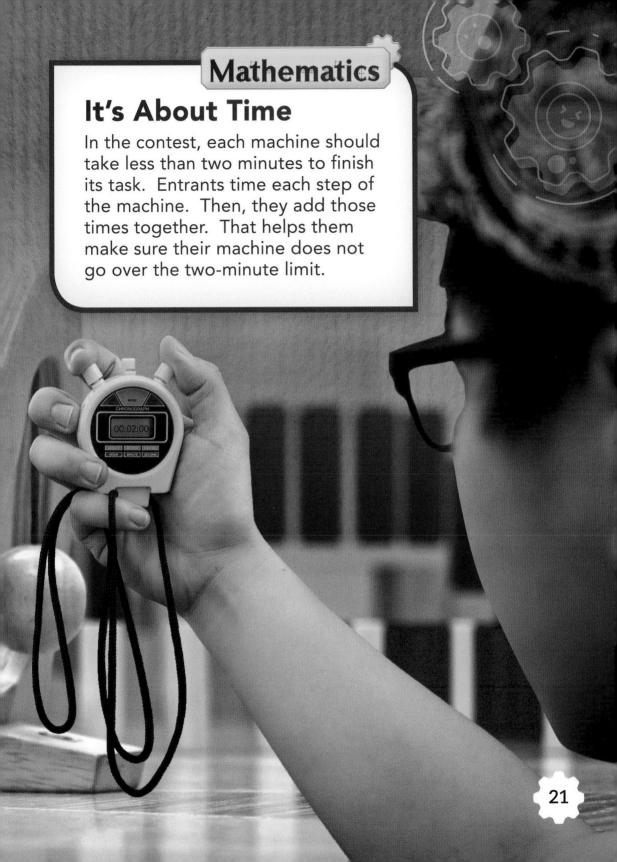

It's About Time

In the contest, each machine should take less than two minutes to finish its task. Entrants time each step of the machine. Then, they add those times together. That helps them make sure their machine does not go over the two-minute limit.

CHRONOGRAPH
00:02:00

The Right Stuff

Entrants need the right items to make fun machines. They must figure out what items can do. They must learn about causes and effects. Entrants must also know how the items respond to force. People can change force to change an effect.

The items used in the contests are common. The fun is in how they go together! Most machines use balls and string. Others use boxes and tubes. They use simple toys, such as cars and blocks, too. Anything can be used. It just needs to do a job in the machine.

A boxing glove pushes a bowling ball down an inclined plane to push a bowling pin.

This Rube Goldberg Machine turns on a light.

23

Each item in a machine is set in motion in its own way. It must apply enough force to move the next item. That is important! The machine only works because each part puts the next part in motion. It works through cause and effect.

Imagine a marble rolls down a tube. At the bottom, the force from the moving marble causes a toy soldier to fall. The toy pushes a block. The block tips onto a lever. The lever tosses a coin in the air. The coin lands in a cup on a spring. The spring is pushed down…and on and on.

Making Movies

Goldberg once wrote a movie script called *Soup to Nuts*. It showed the Three Stooges for the first time. The Three Stooges became very famous characters. They were known for their cause-and-effect pranks.

RUBE GOLDBERG'S all laughing movietone farce..

SOUP TO NUTS

WITH TED HEALY · FRANCES M'COY · STANLEY SMITH · CHARLES WINNINGER

FOX PICTURE

Can You Build One?

Can anyone make a Rube Goldberg Machine? Yes! It takes a lot of creativity and plenty of patience, though!

To draw a machine is one thing. To make it work in real life is another. Each part must work well and the same way every time. The important thing is that the machine completes a final task in a complex way. That is what makes it so much fun! And maybe it would make Rube Goldberg a little proud as well.

Students compete in a Rube Goldberg Machine Contest.

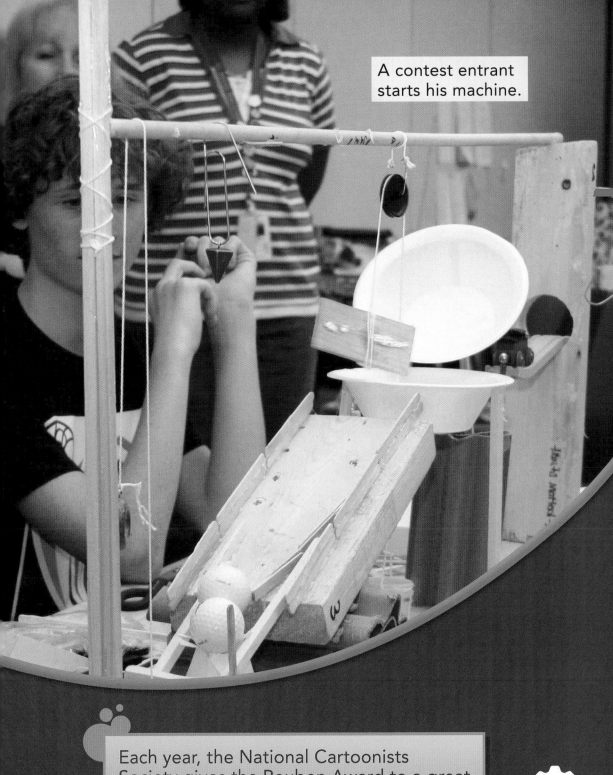

A contest entrant starts his machine.

Each year, the National Cartoonists Society gives the Reuben Award to a great cartoonist. It is named after Goldberg.

STEAM CHALLENGE

Define the Problem

Create and test a machine for a mini Rube Goldberg Machine Contest.

Constraints: You must assemble your machine in 20 minutes or less.

Criteria: Your machine must flip a coin into a cup in less than two minutes. It must be made of at least two simple machines.

Research and Brainstorm

What are examples of simple machines? How do they help make compound machines?

Design and Build

Work with a group to plan your machine. What purpose will each part serve? What materials will work best? Build your model in 20 minutes or less.

Test and Improve

Test your machine. Did the coin land in the cup? Did it take less than two minutes to finish its task? How can you improve it? Improve your design and try again.

Reflect and Share

What was the hardest part about building your machine? Could you have used more simple machines in your model? Would it have made it more or less successful?

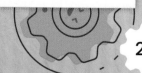

Glossary

balance—a point where something is steady because weight is spread equally on all sides

cartoonist—someone who draws things as a way of saying or doing something

complex—not simple; not easy to explain or understand

compound—formed by combining two or more parts

engineer—a person who uses science to design solutions for problems or needs

entrants—people who enter contests or competitions

national—from all areas of a single country

Pulitzer Prize—one of a group of awards in the United States given each year for excellent work in reporting, writing, or written music

shaft—a long, narrow part of a tool

sloping—slanting upward or downward

Index

Career Advice
from Smithsonian

Do you want to build a Rube Goldberg Machine? Here are some tips to get you started.

"Explore how things work. Read books about machines to learn how to think creatively."—*Tim Pula, Interpretive Exhibit Inventor*

"Take things apart, but don't use a hammer! Then, have fun putting them back together. That will teach you more about how simple machines work together."—*Arthur Daemmrich, Jerome and Dorothy Lemelson Director*